AMAZING SUPER SIMPLE INVENTIONS

SUPER SIMPLE

CAMERA
PROJECTS

INSPIRING & EDUCATIONAL
SCIENCE ACTIVITIES

ALEX KUSKOWSKI

Consulting Editor, Diane Craig, M.A./Reading Specialist

Super Sandcastle

An Imprint of Abdo Publishing
abdopublishing.com

abdopublishing.com

Published by Abdo Publishing, a division of ABDO, PO Box 398166, Minneapolis, Minnesota 55439. Copyright © 2016 by Abdo Consulting Group, Inc. International copyrights reserved in all countries. No part of this book may be reproduced in any form without written permission from the publisher. Super SandCastle™ is a trademark and logo of Abdo Publishing.

Printed in the United States of America, North Mankato, Minnesota
062015
092015

Editor: Liz Salzmann
Content Developer: Nancy Tuminelly
Cover and Interior Design and Production: Mighty Media, Inc.
Photo Credits: Library of Congress, Mighty Media, Inc., Shutterstock, Wikicommons

The following manufacturers/names appearing in this book are trademarks:
Canon® PowerShot®, Yaley™ Gel Wax™, Olympus®, TEDCO Toys®

Library of Congress Cataloging-in-Publication Data

Kuskowski, Alex, author.
  Super simple camera projects : inspiring & educational science activities / Alex Kuskowski ; consulting editor, Diane Craig, M.A./Reading specialist.
      pages cm -- (Amazing super simple inventions)
  Audience: K to grade 4.
  ISBN 978-1-62403-730-6
1. Cameras--Experiments--Juvenile literature. 2. Photography--Equipment and supplies--Juvenile literature. 3. Photography--History--Juvenile literature. I. Craig, Diane, editor. II. Title. III. Series: Kuskowski, Alex. Amazing super simple inventions.
  TR250.K87 2016
  771.3--dc23
                        2014049931

Super SandCastle™ books are created by a team of professional educators, reading specialists, and content developers around five essential components—phonemic awareness, phonics, vocabulary, text comprehension, and fluency—to assist young readers as they develop reading skills and strategies and increase their general knowledge. All books are written, reviewed, and leveled for guided reading and early reading intervention programs for use in shared, guided, and independent reading and writing activities to support a balanced approach to literacy instruction.

To Adult Helpers

The projects in this title are fun and simple. There are just a few things to remember to keep kids safe. Some projects require the use of sharp or hot objects. Also, kids may be using messy materials such as glue. Make sure they protect their clothes and work surfaces. Review the projects before starting, and be ready to assist when necessary.

....

KEY SYMBOLS

Watch for these warning symbols in this book. Here is what they mean.

HOT!
You will be working with something hot. Get help!

SHARP!
You will be working with a sharp object. Get help!

CONTENTS

CAMERAS

AN INTRODUCTION

Say cheese! Cameras were invented more than 200 years ago! They record images that can be saved to look at later.

Pictures once took a long time to make. And they were very expensive. Today we can have a picture in seconds! Thank George Eastman for that. He made taking pictures easy for everyone.

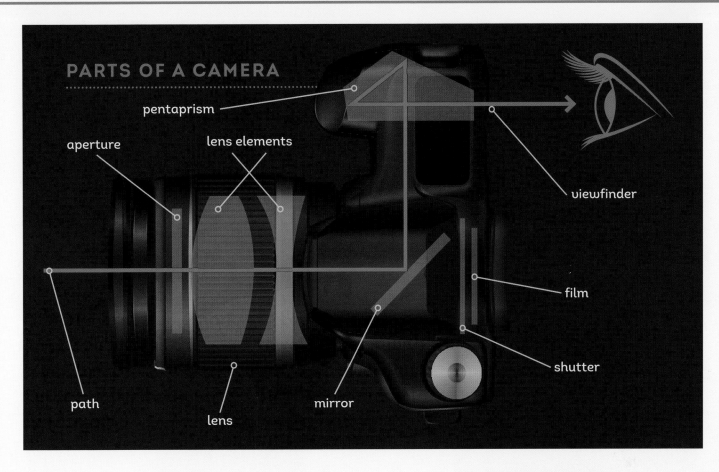

PARTS OF A CAMERA

- pentaprism
- aperture
- lens elements
- viewfinder
- path
- lens
- mirror
- film
- shutter

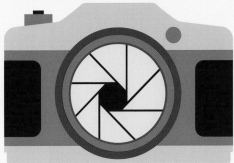

Find out more about Eastman. Learn how cameras work. Discover the invention of photography for yourself!

CAMERA INNOVATORS

GEORGE EASTMAN

Eastman was an **innovator** of the camera. He made photographic film. It was easy to carry. It worked fast.

He formed the Eastman Kodak Company. Many people were able to take photos with his innovations!

The first **innovator** of the camera was Louis Daguerre. He was the first to make a **permanent** image. For each photo, he aimed the camera at one spot for 30 minutes. He had to carry around a lot of heavy **equipment** to take photos.

OTHER IMPORTANT PEOPLE

ALHAZEN

He used a pinhole camera to draw images.

JOSEPH NIÉPCE

He made photos using the sun.

THOMAS EDISON

He was one of the first to use a camera to make a movie.

THEN TO NOW

A TIMELINE OF THE CAMERA

Alhazen was the first person to use a pinhole camera to copy an image.

Louis Daguerre made the first photo that did not fade.

George Eastman invented paper photographic film. He called his camera company Eastman Kodak.

1000   **1816**   **1837**   **1861**   **1884**

Joseph Niépce took the first photo with a camera. It soon faded.

The first color photograph was taken. It was of a tartan ribbon.

The first photographs took a long time to **develop**. People had to sit very still for up to ten minutes! If they moved, they looked blurry in the picture.

Polaroid made the first instant cameras.

The first digital cameras were sold to the public.

1941   **1973**   **1980**   **1990**   **2000**

The first popular **camcorder** was sold. People could record events in their lives in movies.

The first camera phone was sold in Japan. Camera phones quickly spread around the world.

Eastman Kodak made color film. Anyone could take color photos.

BE AN INVENTOR

LEARN HOW TO THINK LIKE AN INVENTOR!

Inventors have a special way of working. It is a series of steps called the Scientific Method. Follow the steps to work like an inventor.

THE SCIENTIFIC METHOD

1. QUESTION

What question are you trying to answer? Write down the question.

2. GUESS

Try to guess the answer to your question. Write down your guess.

3. EXPERIMENT

Think of a way to find the answer. Write down the steps.

KEEP TRACK

There's another way to be just like an inventor. Inventors make notes about everything they do. So get a notebook. When you do an experiment, write down what happens in each step. It's super simple!

4. MATERIALS

What supplies will you need? Make a list.

5. ANALYSIS

Do the experiment. What happened? Write down the results.

6. CONCLUSION

Was your guess correct? Why or why not?

MATERIALS

8 x 8-inch baking pan

baking sheet

camera

card stock

clear glass pane

clear tape

electrical tape

gel wax

lamp

laser pointer

leaves & flowers

lemon juice

Here are some of the **materials** that you will need.

metal sheet

reading glasses

ruler

saucepan

scissors

shoe box

sun-sensitive paper

thumb tack

toilet paper tube

towels

tracing paper

waxed paper

GEL LENSES

Work out how light makes pictures!

MATERIALS: 8 × 8-inch baking pan, waxed paper, gel wax (23 ounces), saucepan, metal sheet, ruler, scissors, laser pointer

Reflection is when light **bounces** off of things. Refraction is when light bends. Cameras use both reflection and refraction.

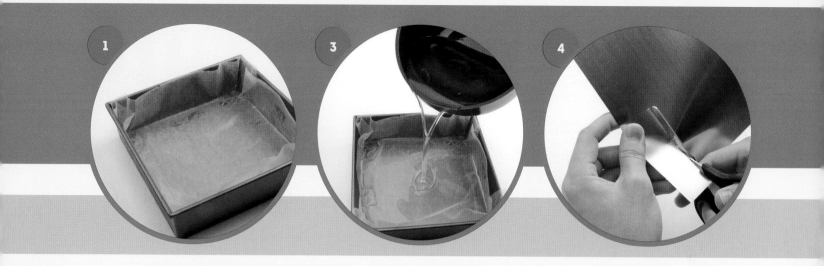

MAKE GEL LENSES

1 Line the baking pan with waxed paper.

2 Melt the gel wax in the saucepan. Follow the instructions on the package.

3 Pour the melted gel wax into the baking pan. Let it cool according to the instructions on the package. Lift the waxed paper to remove the gel wax from the pan.

4 Cut three strips out of the metal sheet. Make them 1 inch (2.5 cm) by 6 inches (15 cm).

continued on next page

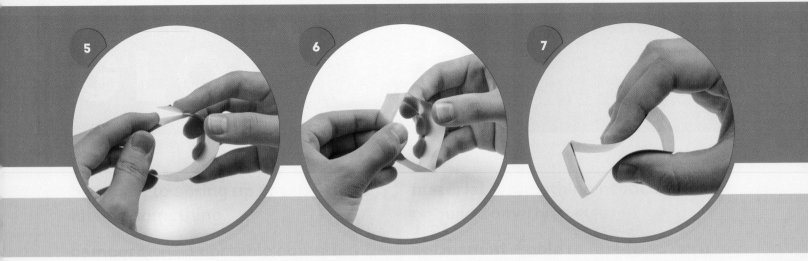

MAKE GEL LENSES (CONTINUED)

5 Bend a metal strip into a circle. Tape the ends together. Press the sides together to flatten the circle. Then pull the sides apart to make a football shape.

6 Repeat step 5 with another metal strip. Make it a different width than the first shape.

7 Bend the third metal strip into a rectangle. Tape the ends together. Pinch the long sides of the rectangle together slightly.

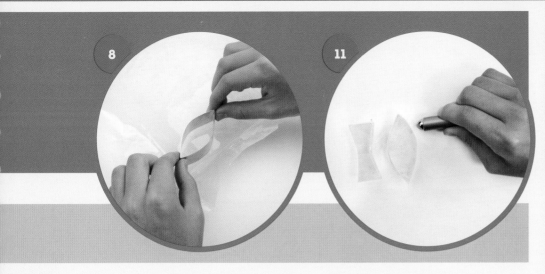

8 Press the metal shapes into the gel wax to cut out gel lenses. Peel the waxed paper away from the gel wax shapes.

9 Lay the lenses flat on a table. Dim the lights.

10 Shine the laser pointer through the side of each lens. Watch what happens to the beam of light. Is it the same for each shape?

11 Put two lenses next to each other. Shine the laser through both the lenses. What happened this time?

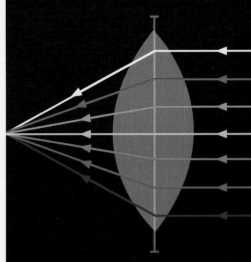

HOW DOES IT WORK?

The lenses you made work like a camera lens. When light goes into a camera, it refracts. It makes the photo bigger or smaller. Light also refracts in the lenses you made.

SUN PRINTS

Create a sun photo!

MATERIALS: leaves and flowers, sun-sensitive paper, baking sheet, clear glass pane, clear tape, water, lemon juice, 2 towels, large book

Heliography was an early photo printing process. The word means *sun drawing*. The first photo was made using heliography.

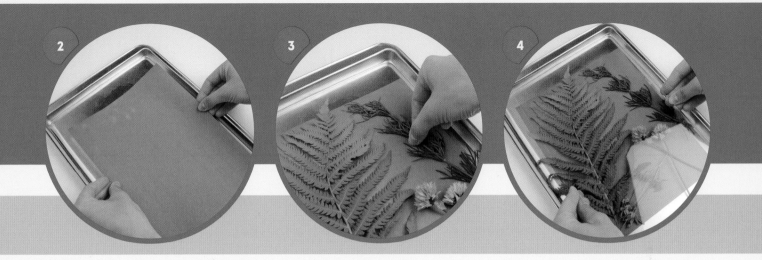

MAKE SUN PRINTS

1 Collect some leaves and flowers. Make sure they will lay flat.

2 Dim the lights. Place a sheet of sun-sensitive paper in a baking pan.

3 Put the leaves and flowers on the paper.

4 Put the glass pane over the leaves and flowers.

continued on next page

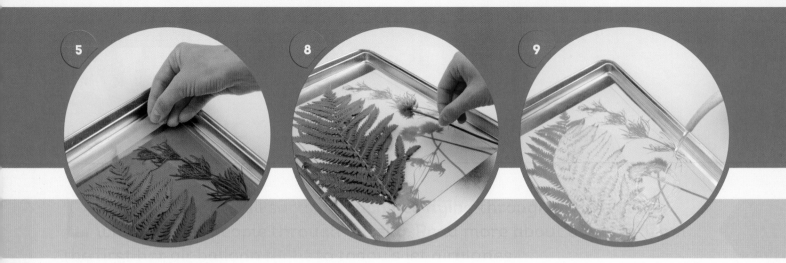

MAKE SUN PRINTS (CONTINUED)

5 Tape the edges of the pane to the baking pan.

6 Carefully pick up the baking pan. Place it in a sunny spot.

7 Wait for 5 minutes or until the paper turns light blue. Remove the baking pan from the sunlight. Take off the tape. Remove the glass.

8 Carefully remove the leaves and flowers.

9 Fill the baking pan with water.

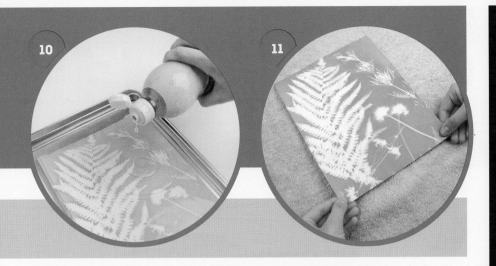

10 Add 3 drops of lemon juice. This makes the blue paper darker. Let the paper **soak** for 1 minute.

11 Lay the paper on a **towel**. Cover it with another towel. Put a large book on top to keep it flat. Check it after 3 days.

Sun-sensitive paper makes a type of heliograph. The sun's rays change the color of the paper. Objects put between the sun and the paper make a picture.

PINHOLE CAMERA

Make the first camera ever!

MATERIALS: shoe box, pencil, tracing paper, ruler, scissors, electrical tape, thumb tack, lamp

Hundreds of years ago, people used this trick to look at the world. Artists used pinhole cameras to trace images.

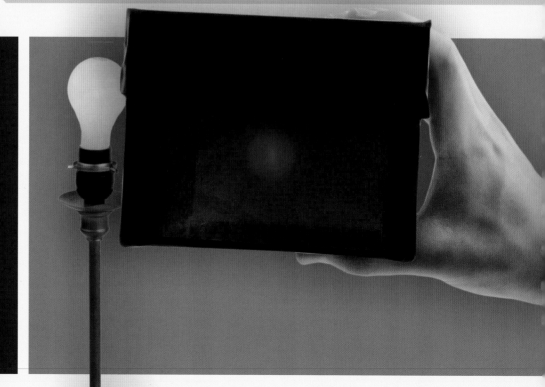

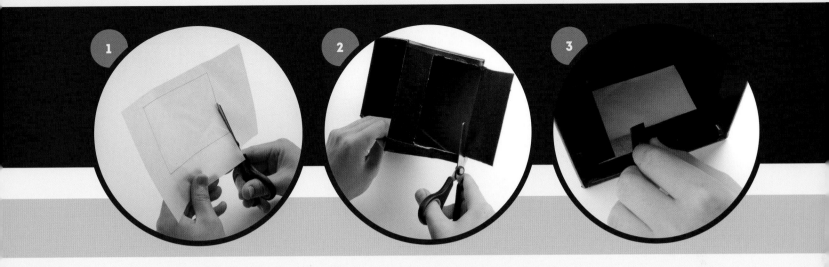

MAKE A PINHOLE CAMERA

1 Draw a rectangle on tracing paper. Make it slightly smaller than the end of the shoe box. Cut it out.

2 Draw a rectangle on the end of the box. Make it slightly smaller than the tracing paper rectangle. Cut it out.

3 Put the tracing paper inside the box. Tape it over the hole you cut out.

continued on next page

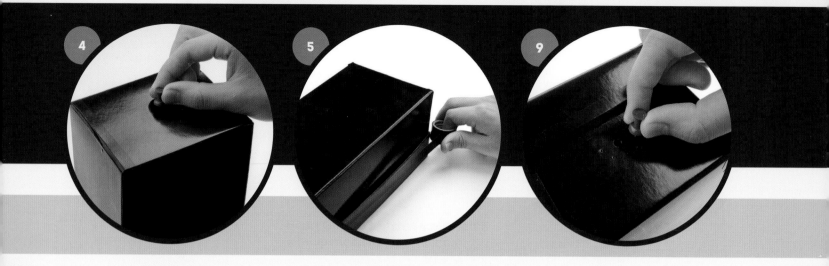

MAKE A PINHOLE CAMERA (CONTINUED)

④ Make a hole in the other end of the box.

⑤ Close the box. Put tape over the edges of the lid.

⑥ Take the shade off of the lamp. Plug it in and turn it on. Do not look directly at the lamp.

⑦ Turn off all other lights. Hold the pinhole camera with the pinhole facing the bulb. Look through the tracing paper window.

⑧ Make the hole larger. Look through the pinhole camera again.

⑨ Make more small holes with the tack. Make them in a circle around the large hole. Make sure the small holes are close to the large hole. Look through the pinhole camera again.

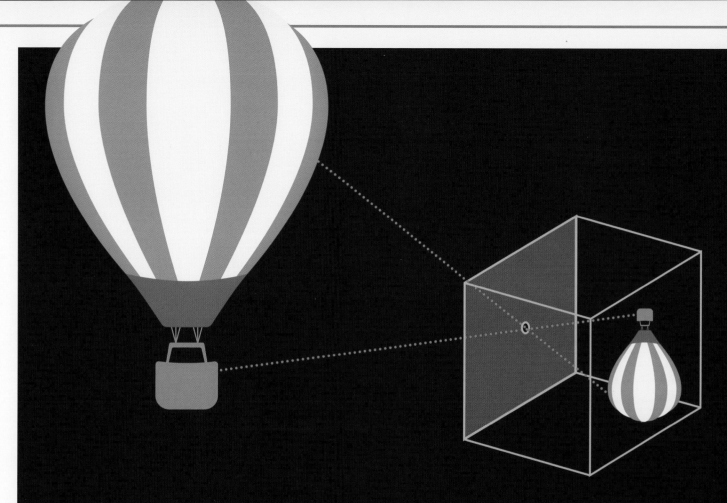

HOW DOES IT WORK?

Pinhole cameras were the first cameras. When light passes through a small hole into a dark area, an image can form. The image will be backwards and upside down.

STEREOSCOPE

See your pictures in 3-D!

MATERIALS: 2 toilet paper tubes, card stock, scissors, clear tape, reading glasses, pencil, ruler, craft glue, camera, printer

Stereoscopes were very popular right after photography was invented. People loved to look at pictures in 3-D.

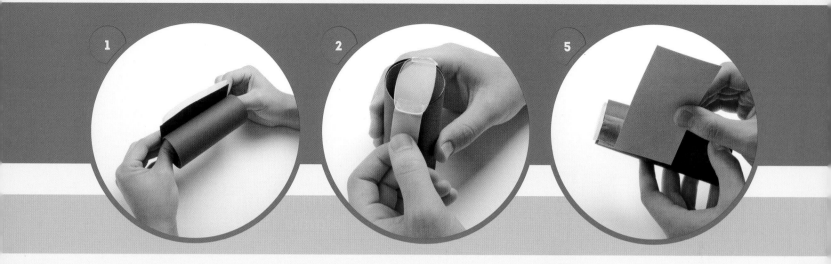

MAKE A STEREOSCOPE

1 Cover the toilet paper tubes with card stock. Tape the ends down.

2 Pop the lenses out of the reading glasses. Tape a lens to one end of each paper tube. Face the fronts of the lenses into the tubes.

3 Write an *L* inside the tube with the left lens. Write an *R* inside the tube with the right lens.

4 Cut a rectangle out of card stock. Make it 2 inches (5 cm) by 4 inches (10 cm).

5 Hold the right lens facing away from you. Make sure the lens is right side up. Glue a short end of the rectangle to the left side of the tube. Place it ½ inch (1.3 cm) from the lens. Add tape for extra support.

continued on next page

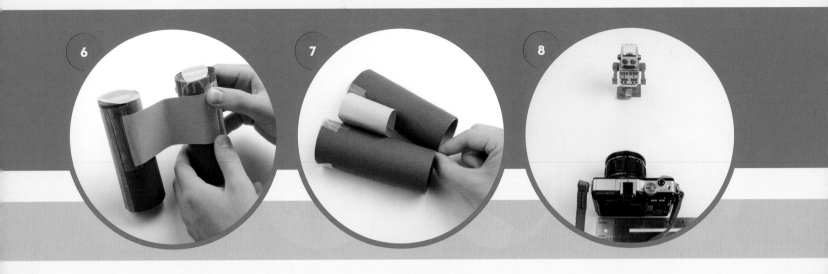

MAKE A STEREOSCOPE (CONTINUED)

6 Hold the left lens facing away from you. Make sure the lens is right side up. Glue the other end of the rectangle to the right side of the tube. Place it ½ inch (1.3 cm) from the lens. Add tape for extra support.

7 Turn the tubes over. Glue the open ends of the tubes together.

8 Choose an object you want to see in 3-D. Take a picture of it. Make sure the object is in the middle of the picture.

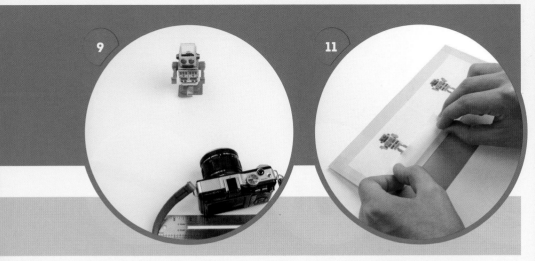

9 Move the camera 2½ inches (6.35 cm) to the right. Turn the camera so the object is centered. Take a picture.

10 Print both pictures 4 inches (10 cm) high and 6 inches (15 cm) wide.

11 Tape the pictures side by side to a piece of card stock. Put the first photo you took on the right side.

12 Set the pictures about 24 inches (61 cm) away from you. Look at them through the lenses.

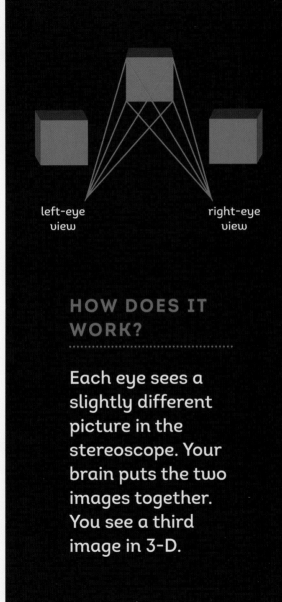

left-eye view

right-eye view

HOW DOES IT WORK?

Each eye sees a slightly different picture in the stereoscope. Your brain puts the two images together. You see a third image in 3-D.

CONCLUSION

Photography is part of daily life. Cameras are everywhere, but do you know how they really work? This book is the first step in discovering what's behind the lens. There is a lot more to find out.

Learn about different types of photography. Look online or at the library. Think of camera crafts and experiments you can do on your own.

Put on your scientist thinking cap and go on a learning journey!

QUIZ

1. How long did Daguerre's camera have to focus on a spot to make a photo?

2. George Eastman took the first photo. **TRUE OR FALSE?**

3. What does heliography mean?

THINK ABOUT IT!

What photo is most important to you? Why?

Answers: 1. 30 minutes   2. False   3. Sun drawing

GLOSSARY

bounce – to spring up or back after hitting something.

camcorder – a portable camera that can take movies and play them back.

develop – to turn film into photographs.

equipment – a set of tools or items used for a special purpose or activity.

innovation – a new way of doing something. Someone who does something in a new way is an innovator.

material – something needed to make or build something else.

permanent – able to last for a very long time.

soak – to remain covered in a liquid for a while.

towel – a cloth or paper used for cleaning or drying.